THE BRIDGE

STUDY GUIDE

Copyright © 2021 by Xavier Cornejo

Published by AVAIL

All rights reserved. No portion of this book may be reproduced, stored in a retrieval system, or transmitted in any form or by any means—electronic, mechanical, photocopy, recording, scanning, or other—except for brief quotations in critical reviews or articles, without prior written permission of the author.

Scripture quotations marked NIV are taken from the Holy Bible, New International Version®, NIV®. Copyright © 1973, 1978, 1984, 2011 by Biblica, Inc.™ Used by permission of Zondervan. All rights reserved worldwide. www.zondervan.com. The "NIV" and "New International Version" are trademarks registered in the United States Patent and Trademark Office by Biblica, Inc.™ Scripture quotations marked NLT are taken from the *Holy Bible*, New Living Translation, copyright © 1996, 2004, 2015 by Tyndale House Foundation. Used by permission of Tyndale House Publishers, Inc., Carol Stream, Illinois 60188. All rights reserved. | The ESV® Bible (The Holy Bible, English Standard Version®). ESV® Text Edition: 2016. Copyright © 2001 by Crossway, a publishing ministry of Good News Publishers. The ESV® text has been reproduced in cooperation with and by permission of Good News Publishers. Unauthorized reproduction of this publication is prohibited. All rights reserved

For foreign and subsidiary rights, contact the author.

Design by Felipe Paredes
Cover Designed by Becky Speer
Illustrations by Xavier Cuenca
Photography by Andrew van Tilborgh

ISBN: 978-1-954089-11-2   1 2 3 4 5 6 7 8 9 10

Printed in the United States of America

XAVIER CORNEJO

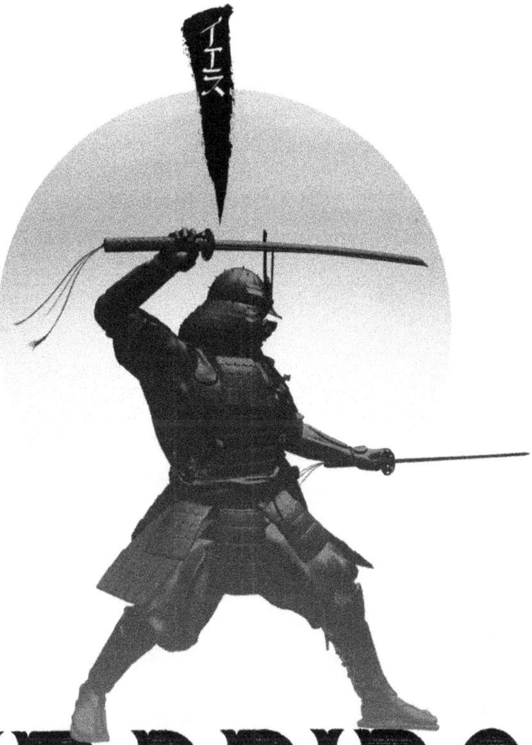

THE BRIDGE
From Possibility to Reality

STUDY GUIDE

Contents

INTRODUCTION 6

1. STRATEGY 12
2. CLARITY 18
3. PEOPLE 24
4. PLANNING 30
5. PREPARATION 36
6. TIME 42
7. EXECUTION 48
8. EVALUATION 54
9. THE PAIN IN THE PATH 60
10. GROWTH 66

Introduction

NEVER GO TO WAR WITHOUT A STRATEGY.

— XAVIER CORNEJO

MAY OUR FOOTPRINTS NOT ONLY TAKE US TO OUR DESTINY, BUT MAY THEY ALSO FORGE A TRAIL FOR OTHERS TO FOLLOW.

REVIEW, REFLECT, AND RESPOND

As you read "Introduction" in *The Bridge*, review, reflect on, and respond to the text by answering the following questions.

What battles exhaust you when you simply think about fighting them?

___

What sparks a flame in you when you feel like you have exhausted all of your inner resources to engage in battle?

___

What talents do you take into life's daily battles with you?

_____
_____
_____
_____
_____
_____
_____

Beyond talent, what have you relied on in the past to give you strength?

_____
_____
_____
_____
_____
_____
_____

REFLECT ON

Do you not know? Have you not heard? The LORD is the everlasting God, the Creator of the ends of the earth. He will not grow tired or weary, and his understanding no one can fathom. He gives strength to the weary and increases the power of the weak. Even youths grow tired and weary, and young men stumble and fall; but those who hope in the LORD will renew their strength. They will soar on wings like eagles; they will run and not grow weary, they will walk and not be faint.

—Isaiah 40:28-31 (NIV)

Consider Isaiah 40:28-31 and answer the following questions:

What comfort can you take in the truth that God does not grow tired or weary?

_____
_____
_____
_____
_____
_____

When have you had to submit to His understanding because you could not fathom it, and you were exhausted trying to?

_____
_____
_____
_____
_____
_____

How does hoping in the Lord renew a person's strength?

What possibilities are you hoping to turn into realities?

What forward steps have you taken in spite of the uncertainties of the future?

As of this moment, what is on the other side of your bridge?

1
Strategy

STRATEGY IS WHERE I GIVE MY GOALS, MY LONGINGS AND MY DREAMS THE OPPORTUNITY TO COME ALIVE. —XAVIER CORNEJO

THINKING DEEPER INTO THE DETAILS IS THE KEY THAT OPENS THE DOOR TO A BETTER TOMORROW. NO MATTER THE RESOURCES YOU HAVE AT HAND, YOU CAN ALWAYS INCREASE THE RESOURCES YOU HAVE IN YOUR HEAD.

REVIEW, REFLECT, AND RESPOND

As you read "Strategy" in *The Bridge*, review, reflect on, and respond to the text by answering the following questions.

In what areas of life do people strategize? What does that look like?

_____
_____
_____
_____
_____
_____

Whom do you admire for his or her ability to strategize? What has that ability earned for that person?

_____
_____
_____
_____
_____

How would you encourage someone who feels that the years have slipped away, yet his or her dreams have not come to fruition?

_____
_____
_____
_____
_____
_____

Considering what you hope for is waiting on the other side of your bridge, what research have you done to determine how you'll reach it?

_____
_____
_____
_____
_____
_____

Where are you right now in relation to the other side of your bridge?

_____
_____
_____
_____
_____
_____

REFLECT ON

Many are the plans in a person's heart, but it is the LORD's purpose that prevails.

—*Proverbs 19:21 (NIV)*

Consider Proverbs 19:21 and answer the following questions:

What situation can you think of in which detailed plans were put into place, but the endeavor was a failure nonetheless?

_____
_____
_____
_____

How can a person prioritize the Lord's purpose, so any plans that person makes will prevail?

_____
_____
_____
_____

How would you encourage someone who is unsure if his or her pursuits are godly?

_____
_____
_____

What resources do you possess—in your hands and in your head—to lead you toward triumph?

How will boldness and courage help you when you feel like you are not making enough forward progress toward your goal?

What is your attitude toward potential strategy changes? Traditionally, how determined or stubborn have you been when it comes changing your plans?

Whom do you admire for using his or her failure as a tool to success? What is that person's story?

2
Clarity

CLARITY IS THE AIR I NEED TO BREATHE
TO REACH THE MOUNTAIN PEAK.

XAVIER CORNEJO

DEFINING WHAT YOU WANT GIVES YOU THE POWER TO PURSUE IT, BUT MORE IMPORTANTLY, IT GIVES YOU THE STRENGTH TO ACHIEVE IT. IF YOU CANNOT SEE CLEARLY, YOU WILL NEVER CHASE YOUR DREAM CORRECTLY BECAUSE YOU WILL NEVER KNOW WHICH BRIDGE TO CROSS TO REACH YOUR GOAL.

REVIEW, REFLECT, AND RESPOND

As you read "Clarity" in *The Bridge*, review, reflect on, and respond to the text by answering the following questions.

_____
_____
_____

At this point, how would you answer Xavier's questions: "Where do I want to go, and how will I get there?"

_____
_____
_____

What role has imagination played as you've envisioned your bridge, possible routes to reach it, and endeavors to cross it?

_____
_____
_____

What does clarity look like in your mind?

_____
_____
_____
_____
_____
_____
_____

What have you found gives you the most clarity when your way appears dimly lit or the path is ambiguous?

_____
_____
_____
_____
_____
_____
_____
_____

How is people's creativity clouded in times of crisis?

_____
_____
_____
_____
_____
_____
_____

REFLECT ON

I gain understanding from your precepts; therefore I hate every wrong path. Your word is a lamp for my feet, a light on my path.

—Psalm 119:104-105 (NIV)

Consider Psalm 119:104-105 and answer the following questions:

What "wrong paths" might the psalmist be referring to in verse 104?

_____
_____
_____
_____
_____
_____
_____
_____

How does God's Word—the Bible—illuminate a Christ-follower's path, so his or her feet don't stumble?

_____
_____
_____
_____
_____
_____
_____
_____

What clouds might "interfere" with the view of your beautiful mountain's peak?

___

What is your plan for dissipating those clouds?

___

Who in your life helps you maintain physical, mental, emotional, and spiritual clarity? What does that person do, and what are the results?

___

On what do you base God's approval for the future you envision?

___

3
People

UNITY GIVES RISE TO LOYALTY.

XAVIER CORNEJO

MAY YOU ALWAYS HAVE A GENUINE DESIRE TO HELP OTHERS, TO INSPIRE OTHERS, AND ABOVE ALL THINGS, TO SERVE OTHERS. ONLY THEN WILL YOU GENERATE THE IMPACT YOU WANT TO CREATE.

REVIEW, REFLECT, AND RESPOND

As you read "People" in *The Bridge*, review, reflect on, and respond to the text by answering the following questions.

Is your natural inclination to go fast or go far? Go alone or together? What do you see as the strengths and weaknesses of each?

_____
_____
_____
_____
_____

With whom have you chosen to walk toward his or her mission? What has that looked like?

_____
_____
_____
_____
_____

What is your experience with working on a team? Does your experience reflect the evidence?

_____
_____
_____
_____
_____
_____

If the measure of your life will be evaluated based on the number of people you've helped on your way up, on a scale of 0 to 10—0 being none, 10 being many—how do you think people would measure your life? How would you measure your life? Explain your rationale.

_____
_____
_____
_____
_____
_____

When have you and another person chosen to embark on separate journeys? What were the feelings then? How are your feelings about that separation now?

_____
_____
_____
_____
_____
_____

REFLECT ON

Two are better than one, because they have a good return for their labor: If either of them falls down, one can help the other up. But pity anyone who falls and has no one to help them up. Also, if two lie down together, they will keep warm. But how can one keep warm alone? Though one may be overpowered, two can defend themselves. A cord of three strands is not quickly broken.

—Ecclesiastes 4:9-12 (NIV)

Consider Ecclesiastes 4:9-12 and answer the following questions:

What wisdom do you see in these verses?

_____
_____
_____
_____

How did Christ reflect this wisdom in His interactions with people?

_____
_____
_____
_____

How could you encourage someone who is discouraged by a lack of support from family, friends, coworkers, etc.?

_____
_____
_____
_____

What is your greatest challenge when it comes to giving and taking advice?

_____
_____
_____
_____
_____

Who are your most precious treasures? What has caused those people to be so valuable to you?

_____
_____
_____
_____
_____
_____

Whose footprints guide, inspire, and motivate you? What specifically do those people do that impacts you?

_____
_____
_____
_____
_____

What footprints are you attempting to leave for those who follow you?

_____
_____
_____
_____
_____

4
Planning

WHEN IT COMES TO THE BATTLES FOR YOUR GOALS, ANY IDEA CAN BE LIKE A SHARPENED WEAPON

XAVIER CORNEJO

THE FIGHT FOR YOUR GOALS DESERVES YOUR ALL, AND YOU MUST FIGHT WITH ALL YOUR SOUL. IF YOU DO SO, YOU WILL HAVE ALREADY WON.

REVIEW, REFLECT, AND RESPOND

As you read "Planning" in *The Bridge*, review, reflect on, and respond to the text by answering the following questions.

Remind yourself of the following before starting to make your plan:

What place are you attempting to reach?

_____
_____
_____
_____
_____

Who is guiding you or walking with you toward that location?

_____
_____
_____
_____
_____

Xavier asks, "What steps do I need to take to cross the bridge to what I aim to obtain?" and, "What can I do to go from where I am to where I want to go?" What other questions guide your planning?

_____
_____
_____
_____

As you write your ideas, keep in mind that they should inspect the past, inspire the present, and innovate the future.

_____
_____
_____
_____

Which ideas are you tempted to discard? Why does Xavier say you should keep them?

_____
_____
_____
_____

What kind of moments light up your imagination? How might your list of ideas be enhanced if your imagination were lit?

_____
_____
_____
_____

REFLECT ON

Then the LORD said to Joshua, "See, I have delivered Jericho into your hands, along with its king and its fighting men. March around the city once with all the armed men. Do this for six days. Have seven priests carry trumpets of rams' horns in front of the ark. On the seventh day, march around the city seven times, with the priests blowing the trumpets. When you hear them sound a long blast on the trumpets, have the whole army give a loud shout; then the wall of the city will collapse and the army will go up, everyone straight in."

—Joshua 6:2-5 (NIV)

Consider Joshua 6:2-5 and answer the following questions:

What place were the Israelites trying to reach? How was God guiding them to their location?

_____

_____

_____

What would have happened if Joshua had discarded God's plan?

_____

_____

_____

How does God's method for conquering Jericho encourage you to consider every possible route to and across your bridge?

_____

_____

_____

_____

What resources—physical, emotional, and financial—do you feel you are lacking? What role will potential play as you consider ways to make up for the need?

_____
_____
_____
_____

When has it seemed like an opportunity has passed you by, but a better tomorrow was on the horizon?

_____
_____
_____
_____

Xavier only regrets the defeats he suffered because he gave up. How do you deal with defeat?

_____
_____
_____
_____

Think of different ways your plans to reach and cross your bridge can fail. List two to five solutions for each of those issues.

_____
_____
_____
_____

Preparation

THE LEVEL OF YOUR PREPARATION DETERMINES
THE LEVEL OF YOUR ELEVATION.

— XAVIER CORNEJO

WHAT ARE YOU DOING TODAY FOR YOUR TOMORROW? WHAT ARE YOU PREPARING YOURSELF FOR? IF YOU KNOW WHAT YOU WANT AND HOW TO OBTAIN IT, YOU NEED PREPARATION TO ATTAIN IT.

REVIEW, REFLECT, AND RESPOND

As you read "Preparation" in *The Bridge*, review, reflect on, and respond to the text by answering the following questions.

Whom do you admire who consistently trains to reach his or her goals? What has been the outcome of the training?

_____
_____
_____
_____
_____

How have you prepared yourself to win some of the battles you've fought in your past?

_____
_____
_____
_____
_____
_____

Xavier believes that goals are not reached in a day. Instead, they are reached daily. What is the difference? What goals do you attempt to reach daily?

_____
_____
_____
_____
_____
_____
_____
_____

How great is your willingness to know and your disposition to grow?

_____
_____
_____
_____
_____
_____
_____
_____

Do you prefer thinking or fighting? Why is it imperative you develop both skills as you pursue your destiny?

_____
_____
_____
_____
_____
_____
_____
_____

REFLECT ON

Run in such a way as to get the prize. Everyone who competes in the games goes into strict training. They do it to get a crown that will not last, but we do it to get a crown that will last forever. Therefore I do not run like someone running aimlessly; I do not fight like a boxer beating the air. No, I strike a blow to my body and make it my slave so that after I have preached to others, I myself will not be disqualified for the prize.

—*1 Corinthians 9:24-27 (NIV)*

Consider 1 Corinthians 9:24-27 and answer the following questions:

When are you tempted to simply run the race or play the game instead of aiming for the prize?

_____
_____
_____
_____
_____

What does it look like when someone is running aimlessly or boxing the air? How can that imagery be applied to the pursuit of one's dream?

_____
_____
_____
_____
_____
_____

In what ways might you have to make your body—including your heart and mind—your slave?

_____
_____
_____
_____

Whom do you know who has had to reinvent him or herself because the original invention didn't fulfill its purpose? What were the results of the reinvention?

___

What critical places do you expect to encounter in your passage toward your bridge? What is your plan to get past them?

___

Where can you find the glory of victory in your daily routine?

___

How can you be intentional as you not only plan but also prepare to reach your bridge?

___

6
Time

> MAY TIME NOT BE THE ONLY ONE TO LEAVE ITS MARK IN YOU; MAY YOU ALSO LEAVE YOUR MARK IN TIME.
> XAVIER CORNEJO

DON'T WORRY ABOUT YESTERDAY. WORRY ABOUT WHAT YOU WILL DO TODAY TO REACH THE PLACE THAT IN YOUR TOMORROW YOU LONG FOR. THE PAST HAS NEVER DEFINED A PERSON; ONLY ONE'S DAILY DECISIONS CAN DO THAT.

REVIEW, REFLECT, AND RESPOND

As you read "Time" in *The Bridge*, review, reflect on, and respond to the text by answering the following questions.

How do you view time—its quantity, speed, value, etc.?

_____
_____
_____
_____
_____

How well do you master your time? On what criteria do you base your assessment?

_____
_____
_____
_____
_____

How could you encourage someone who feels like he or she never has enough time or doesn't know where the time has gone?

_____
_____
_____
_____
_____

How can a person balance living in the moment with keeping in mind what he or she desires to obtain over time?

_____
_____
_____
_____
_____

How much time are you anticipating it will take you to reach and cross your bridge? How are you preparing yourself to make the most of that time?

_____
_____
_____
_____
_____

> ## REFLECT ON
>
> *For everything there is a season, a time for every activity under heaven. A time to be born and a time to die. A time to plant and a time to harvest. A time to kill and a time to heal. A time to tear down and a time to build up.*
>
> —*Ecclesiastes 3:1-3 (NLT)*

Consider Ecclesiastes 3:1-3 and answer the following questions:

Why do you think King Solomon chose extremes when he reflected on time?

_____
_____
_____
_____

How can his words help you when you are feeling desperate to reach your goal?

_____
_____
_____
_____

Conversely, why might it be appropriate—as Xavier believes—to grow desperate to maintain the rhythm of your walk?

_____
_____
_____
_____

How can you protect yourself over time, so you are not frustrated when it seems like important moments have passed?

_____
_____
_____
_____
_____
_____

What do you feel is going to be the wisest investment of your time in the present, so you can maintain rhythm in your daily walk?

_____
_____
_____
_____
_____
_____

How might your physical, emotional, and spiritual well-being be compromised if you don't maintain rhythm in your daily walk?

_____
_____
_____
_____
_____
_____

1
Execution

> WHEN WE MASTER EXECUTION,
> WE WILL MASTER VICTORY.
>
> XAVIER CORNEJO

HOW MANY IDEAS OR PLANS HAVE YOU HAD THAT REMAINED SIMPLY IDEAS AND PLANS? WHERE DID THEY GO WRONG? WAS IT THE IDEA? WAS IT THE PLANNING? OR WAS IT THAT YOU NEVER EXECUTED THEM?

REVIEW, REFLECT, AND RESPOND

As you read "Execution" in *The Bridge*, review, reflect on, and respond to the text by answering the following questions.

Who can you think of from history or present day who made great plans but never delivered on them? What happened?

_____
_____
_____
_____
_____

What plans have you made that never materialized? What prevented them from coming to fruition?

_____
_____
_____
_____
_____

Traditionally, how have you dealt with your or someone else's inability to accomplish a goal?

___

Troubleshoot ways in which Xavier's "Enemies of Execution" could prevent you from crossing your bridge?

Too many opportunities

___

Lack of effectiveness

___

Distractions

___

Delaying

___

Lack of motivation

___

REFLECT ON

For which of you, desiring to build a tower, does not first sit down and count the cost, whether he has enough to complete it? Otherwise, when he has laid a foundation and is not able to finish, all who see it begin to mock him, saying, "This man began to build and was not able to finish." Or what king, going out to encounter another king in war, will not sit down first and deliberate whether he is able with ten thousand to meet him who comes against him with twenty thousand?

—Luke 14: 28-31 (ESV)

Although Luke 14:28-31 focuses primarily on external resources, consider them in Xavier's context and answer the following questions:

What prevented the builder from completing his tower? How could the builder have prevented this and ended up with better results?

_____
_____
_____

What is the king having to consider? How is his decision going to affect others in addition to himself?

_____
_____
_____

How can these situations involving external resources be applied to your desire to cross your bridge?

_____
_____
_____

Ask yourself the three questions: Who? What? and When? How do their answers lend themselves to your walking toward and crossing your bridge?

_____
_____
_____
_____

How do you respond to pressure? If Xavier is right, and "today's pressure is tomorrow's precision," how can you make pressure work for you?

_____
_____
_____
_____

Whom can you enlist to hold you accountable to keep moving forward toward your bridge? How can this person or these people help you?

What excuses do you hear are most commonly given for failure? How do they reflect a willingness (or unwillingness) to take ownership of one's actions (or lack of action)?

How would you encourage someone who feels like failure is the norm but desperately wants to reach and cross a bridge?

Evaluation

> YOU CAN ONLY RISE FROM THE ASHES
> WHEN YOU EVALUATE WHY YOU GOT BURNED.
>
> XAVIER CORNEJO

THE BEAUTY OF LIFE IS NOT FOUND ONLY IN THE GREATEST MOMENTS THAT MAY COME OUR WAY, BUT ALSO IN THE SMALL DETAILS OF EVERY DAY. IF WE DO NOT EVALUATE OUR DAYS, WE MAY MISS THE BEAUTIFUL MOMENTS THAT SILENTLY WAITED THERE.

REVIEW, REFLECT, AND RESPOND

As you read "Evaluation" in *The Bridge*, review, reflect on, and respond to the text by answering the following questions.

When have you or someone you know felt like Adonis Creed and reflected, "I don't even know how I lost?"

_____
_____
_____
_____
_____
_____

What ended up being the reason for the lack of success?

_____
_____
_____
_____
_____
_____

How did the situation get redeemed; how did the path get found again?

What effective methods of evaluation have you or the people walking with you implemented? How do those methods change with different circumstances?

How would you encourage someone who feels like assessment and evaluation are forms of criticism?

REFLECT ON

"Lord, have mercy on my son. He has seizures and suffers terribly. He often falls into the fire or into the water. So I brought him to your disciples, but they couldn't heal him ..."

Afterward the disciples asked Jesus privately, "Why couldn't we cast out that demon?"

"You don't have enough faith," Jesus told them.

—Matthew 17:15-16, 19-20 (NLT)

Consider Matthew 17:15-16, 19-20 and answer the following questions:

What situation caused the disciples to evaluate their methods for fulfilling the call on their lives?

_____
_____
_____

How did they go about the evaluation?

_____
_____
_____
_____

What options did they have once Jesus revealed to them the secret to their failure?

_____
_____
_____

As you execute your plan to reach and cross your bridge, how and when are you planning to evaluate your progress?

How could answering the questions, "How did I get here?" and, "Am I where I want to be?" assist you?

To whom can you go to ask for honest reflection regarding your progress and realistic adjustments to further it?

When you've exhausted your earthly resources, what comfort can you take from James 1:5 (NIV): "If any of you lacks wisdom, you should ask God, who gives generously to all without finding fault, and it will be given to you"?

9
The Pain in the Path

WHAT MAKES YOU A WINNER IS WALKING DESPITE THE PAIN.
XAVIER CORNEJO

THE STORIES, MOVIES OR NOVELS THAT WE FIND CAPTIVATING ARE NOT THE ONES WHERE EVERYTHING CAME EASILY; THEY ARE THE ONES IN WHICH THE CHARACTERS OVERCOME THE DARKEST AND IRREMEDIABLE MOMENTS THAT MAKE THEIR HEARTS ACHE DEEPLY.

REVIEW, REFLECT, AND RESPOND

As you read "The Pain in the Path" in *The Bridge*, review, reflect on, and respond to the text by answering the following questions.

Who do you know who has suffered greatly on his or her path toward a bridge? How did that person respond to the pain?

_____
_____
_____
_____
_____

What pain have you encountered on your previous paths? What has been your traditional response to it?

_____
_____
_____
_____
_____

How has stagnancy been painful for you or those you know? How is it different from outright pain or fear of failure?

___

What allies have walked, breathed, and waited to accompany you through these types of pain on the pathway to your destiny?

___

What encouragement would you give to someone on the brink of defeat due to his or her overwhelming desire to give up?

___

REFLECT ON

Consider it pure joy, my brothers and sisters, whenever you face trials of many kinds, because you know that the testing of your faith produces perseverance. Let perseverance finish its work so that you may be mature and complete, not lacking anything ... Blessed is the one who perseveres under trial because, having stood the test, that person will receive the crown of life that the Lord has promised to those who love him.

—James 1:2-4, 12 (NIV)

Consider James 1:2-4, 12 and answer the following questions:

How does a person's perspective change when he or she views life's trials as growing or "maturing" pains?

_____
_____
_____

What causes people to have the strength to persevere?

_____
_____
_____
_____

What could joy possibly have to do with trial and testing? What does it look like?

_____
_____
_____
_____

What do the Lord's crown and a person's reaching and crossing his or her bridge have in common?

___

___

___

Describe a situation and its outcome in which a person's pain added beauty to his or her story.

_____
_____
_____
_____

How do you push through the pain and keep walking toward your goals?

_____
_____
_____
_____

Who do you know who has truly made his or her bridge easier to reach because the pain of attaining the further bridge was too much?

_____
_____
_____
_____

What pain do you anticipate encountering on the path toward your particular bridge? What strategies do you plan to implement to push through it?

_____
_____
_____
_____

10
Growth

REACHING OUR GOALS IS IMPORTANT; IT HELPS US HAVE A FULL LIFE. WHAT DEFINES YOU, THOUGH, IS NOT WHAT YOU DO; IT'S WHO YOU ARE. YOU CAN RENOUNCE WHAT YOU DO, BUT YOU CAN'T RENOUNCE WHO YOU ARE. ALL OF YOUR ACHIEVEMENTS CAN FADE AWAY, BUT WHO YOU ARE WILL ALWAYS REMAIN.

REVIEW, REFLECT, AND RESPOND

As you read "Growth" in *The Bridge*, review, reflect on, and respond to the text by answering the following questions.

How do you differentiate between reaching goals in life and having goals that take a lifetime to reach?

_____
_____
_____
_____
_____

What decisions do you make each day to grow and broaden your horizon?

_____
_____
_____
_____
_____
_____

What hope do you find in the research that shows that the human brain can establish new patterns for its dendrite branches when necessary, meaning a person can influence his or her thought patterns?

Do you consider yourself to have a fixed or growth mindset? What behaviors or thought processes lead you to that conclusion?

Who do you know who has an obviously fixed or growth mindset? How is it manifested?

REFLECT ON

Therefore, I urge you, brothers and sisters, in view of God's mercy, to offer your bodies as a living sacrifice, holy and pleasing to God—this is your true and proper worship. Do not conform to the pattern of this world, but be transformed by the renewing of your mind. Then you will be able to test and approve what God's will is—his good, pleasing and perfect will.

—Romans 12:1-2 (NIV)

Consider Romans 12:1-2 and answer the following questions:

How do you traditionally worship?

_____
_____
_____
_____

How can you offer your body as a living sacrifice to God—as a means of true and proper worship—as you follow your path to your bridge?

_____
_____
_____
_____

What will it or does it look like when you renew your mind? How does it lead to growth?

_____
_____
_____
_____

What can you do to nurture your own and other people's curiosity?

_____
_____
_____
_____

What have you learned in an unrelated situation that you can extrapolate into your current situation? How have you applied it?

_____
_____
_____
_____

Despite changing seasons in your life, what part of you has remained the same? What does that part communicate to you about who you are?

_____
_____
_____
_____

How can you nurture the part of you that God has made unique to you, so it grows and flourishes and enables you to reach and cross your bridge?

_____
_____
_____
_____

THERE IS NO BARRIER YOU CANNOT SURPASS, BRIDGE YOU CANNOT CROSS, GOAL YOU CANNOT REACH, BATTLE YOU CANNOT WIN IF YOU JUST DARE TO TRY

www.ingramcontent.com/pod-product-compliance
Lightning Source LLC
Chambersburg PA
CBHW070209100426
42743CB00013B/3107